# Digging a Moose from the Snow

*poems by*

# Skaidrite Stelzer

*Finishing Line Press*
Georgetown, Kentucky

# Digging a Moose from the Snow

Copyright © 2021 by Skaidrite Stelzer
ISBN 978-1-64662-455-3 First Edition
All rights reserved under International and Pan-American Copyright Conventions. No part of this book may be reproduced in any manner whatsoever without written permission from the publisher, except in the case of brief quotations embodied in critical articles and reviews.

## ACKNOWLEDGMENTS

"Bee Pollen," *Muse & Stone* (2007).
"Black Sparrows," in *Glass: A Journal of Poetry*, Volume 6, Issue One, June 2013
"Death of Marius," in *The New Verse News*, February 15, 2014.
"Digging a Moose from the Snow." originally published as "shoveling out a moose," in *New Verse News*, January 5, 2018
"Jay," in *Brickplight*, Issue 2, February 2014
"The Pirushke Lady Warns Me of Going Barefoot," *The Third Coast*, 1976
"The Sorcerer's Daughter," in *New Zoo Poetry Review* (#11), (2007)
"Starfish" in *Cactus Heart*, #10, Winter, 2014

Publisher: Leah Huete de Maines
Editor: Christen Kincaid
Cover Art: Vija Doks
Author Photo: Skai Stelzer Jr.
Cover Design: Elizabeth Maines McCleavy

Printed in the USA on acid-free paper.
Order online: www.finishinglinepress.com
also available on amazon.com

Author inquiries and mail orders:
Finishing Line Press
P. O. Box 1626
Georgetown, Kentucky 40324
U. S. A.

# Table of Contents

The "Pirushke" Lady Warns Me of Going Barefoot ........................ 1

Grasshopper ........................................................................................ 2

Cooper's Hawks in March ................................................................ 3

Death of Marius, February 9, 2014 ................................................ 4

Selected Animals ............................................................................... 5

Black Sparrow ................................................................................... 6

Bee Pollen .......................................................................................... 7

digging a moose from the snow ..................................................... 9

Starfish ............................................................................................. 10

Batty .................................................................................................. 11

The Language of Dolphins ............................................................ 12

Two goats, two stars, one mountain ............................................. 14

Cicada Shells ................................................................................... 15

Gorilla Girl ....................................................................................... 18

Plastic Penguins under Carport ................................................... 19

Jay ..................................................................................................... 20

The Sorcerer's Daughter ................................................................ 21

Elephant ........................................................................................... 22

Sea Lion ........................................................................................... 23

Denali Autumn ............................................................................... 24

Walleye ............................................................................................. 25

just a small dog rescued from the rain ....................................... 26

The First to Die .............................................................................. 27

## The "Pirushke" Lady Warns Me of Going Barefoot

In a few years your arches will fall
your feet grow hooved
toes become turtles
your husband will leave.

## Grasshopper

> *"In a field I am the absence of field"*
> —Mark Strand

That boy was chasing grasshoppers when he was lost;
or swimming in Comstock Lake.
Drowned, he looked foreign.
The absence of self
that calls me back to that empty field,
the imagined home
before crop-dusting.
A low plane casts the silhouette
of starved hawks,
the mice curling sick in developing corn
that will make the syrup
of addiction.
I've always been absent.
The boy holds out the grasshopper.
My finger stains with "tobacco" juice.
Algae chokes the lake.

**Cooper's Hawks in March**

The men from the gas company paint
A green arrow on my pine tree.
It points toward earth,
A language I do not yet grasp.
Thinking there must be a pipe there.
Dreaming a startled explosion.

In the upper branches the Cooper's hawk nests.
The egg-bound female.
Her warning cry wakes me—
The repetitious cackle of a hag's laugh in a movie.

I've watched her struggle with broken twigs,
Leaving the larger below.
Winter's discards—now the damp meals of carpenter ants.

The men will start digging, they say,
In April when the ground is soft.
Will they go under the tree?
Or around?
I contemplate the arrow.

From the ground the nest is invisible,
But I can see it from my upstairs window.
The small male offers red food
Which they toss on the branches
Before swallowing whole.

To make sure it is dead, I think.
Avoiding a struggle inside,
Avoiding the mouse's eye that could suddenly blink.
The Cooper's hawks soar in the clean world,
Circling the unmarked distances.
Their bolted eyes anticipate me
Watching behind the glass.

## Death of Marius, February 9, 2014

In the Copenhagen zoo the children watch
with solemn faces, dressed
in their winter gear, blue hooded,
as Marius the giraffe is shot through his
head with a crushing bolt
and falls dead instantly.
Then the removal of the pelt as
the children's faces,
expressionless,
watch the autopsy and
the meat
appreciated by hungry lions.
The inside of a giraffe has many interlaced
organs. The children learn how they were put
together once.  It is a natural environment. Only
later will they learn the lightness of their own organs,
the human autopsy now vaguely familiar,
an implanted memory.

**Selected Animals**

I dream I have to shoot the bear although
somewhere inside I love the bear.
I've got a dream bestiary in my backyard
—cats, chicken, geese, and maybe a dog or two—
penned in by chicken wire.
They won't survive the night.
I reach for the dream rifle.
Black and shiny, it fits my hand.
I open the door. The bear's eyes
Glow in the night right outside.
I start to shoot, but it isn't a bear.
The bear seems human, someone visiting.
A dead lover perhaps, now returning.
But I've shot it.
It dies as a bear.
All the kittens come out from hiding.
I'm missing two chickens and three geese.

**Black Sparrow**

Near the yellow bush
      where they've gathered
           to punctuate
the winter morning
      with full stops,

I pause.  Their shapes round
      musical notes against the electric wires.
Something smudged
      from a dream sampler.

She bends to try
      on the sister's tap shoes
clacking with bent knees
      on the burned linoleum.

The yellow and green merge.

A black sparrow seems impossible
      unless against the sun.
The way the afterimage lingers,
      the pinch of the toes
           creating the wavering dance.

## Bee Pollen

I think of us buzzing around the room
with stout stomachs and little gauze wings.
In the conversation we circle
until we feel we're getting somewhere.
Or something is getting freed,
if only honey.

Where does the honey lead?
It's too sweet to nourish much
and it sticks to everything
so nothing can come clean.
But we coat the house with it
like a hive.
The cells that lead to births
of workers and drones
but no queens.

Droning is not such a bad habit.
If the words stick to meanings,
haphazardly,
that's really just as well.
Because it's the making
that really counts.
The making and protecting.

There are no king bees,
and we never wonder why.
Sweetness scared them off early
so they didn't develop
their dominion.
Became only stingers
and guards
working on stuff
that can't matter.

Buzzing is the sound
of pleasure
and dreams.
Too much sweetness
glues the eyes open at last.

**digging a moose from the snow**

most of us do what we can
if we believe we can do it
if someone has not whispered in our ears
that the world is too cruel
a world that will kill us (it's true)
yet we must move against the snow banks
dig deeper than we believe

a moose in a snowbank
that in summer would throw us
trampled in grass
now knows we are animal
surviving
all of us
as best we can

**Starfish**

"You will live in the desert without rain."
The prediction of the turbaned man
who confronts me on the beach,
Far Rockaway. He says he is a poet,
will write for coins,
anything you offer is fine.
"You will dry up, your branches lose sap."
He tells me harsh fortunes,
refusing to bloom without money.
I look at the slow foaming waters,
thin upon the sand.
See starfish glitter there,
growing new limbs.

## Batty

The opposite world hangs before you,
reversed like the first world,
before you learned the corrections.

The bat insists on the original.
The eye that opens at night,
red in moonlight.

You run with the flashlight,
watch the swirl of wings circling the pine top,
widening and swooping to your shouts.

Your tennis shoes squeak—
bright echoes that fool you.
You think you are followed.
You hide your long hair.

As at a concert now and then
the bat swoops down
and one woman screams
within the somber cello notes,
the conductor pretending not to notice
the broken music.

You run in the night within the rabid wings,
child to old woman,
wrapped in your cape,
your rubber soled sighs.

## The Language of Dolphins

In the night the dolphin
cries lonely for her who first
taught him language who stroked
his back and taught him the little
he could learn there of sex.

He would swim from room to room
and nuzzle her feet as she hung
suspended slightly out of reach
taking notes at her desk listening
for his intonations.

And then the head scientist went
in other directions finding his
own language in LSD.
And she being only the assistant pleaded
her damp pages of sounds
held to her chest.

The rooms were drained where
he would swim to her
kiss her knees gently in greeting
and she would dive down
to the watery acknowledgement.

He is locked into a cage for transport.
He pounds against it until his
mouth bleeds.  When they release
him everything is square and
empty a tank deemed adequate
for a research subject.

She never comes to visit.
Devastated too by her own bare
rooms.  She lives a dry life now.
Never learns his language.

He doesn't eat for two weeks
and then he dies.

## Two goats, two stars, one mountain

Avoiding the terraces they climb on human construction,
the beams that hold them steady, these Indian mountain goats.
They know rivers and rich boats, the indulgence of bells,
but here things are hewn within stricter elevations,
right angled, while below grow golden flowers,
star-formed, spangling the rock-bound greenery.
The mother and child look straight ahead, untouched
by elevation, a desire for flight does not enclose these
bodies. Instead they are satisfied where they are. Balanced
on human construction that fits as well as more constricting
dreams. They have chosen this elevation without
the need for measurement. Desire matches these hoofs
steady tension. They go exactly where they will.

**Cicada Shells**

The granddaughters string them in long necklaces
before they learn the fear of bugs.

. . . . . . . . . . . . . . . .

Because she knows she'll die that night,
she asks me to help her change to her good
flannel nightgown.
I avert my eyes from the large black mole on her back
which she has hidden all these years.

. . . . . . . . . . . . . . . .

The journalist writes of a severed hand
thinking if it had a ring
he would know it was female.

. . . . . . . . . . . . . . . .

The tank has been designed
without eyes
or any recognizable
human features.

. . . . . . . . . . . . . . . .

She calls me Ti-Ti,
a name she made up.
I pull down the leaves she can't reach yet.

. . . . . . . . . . . . . . . .

I've never held a live one.
Though the cat catches them and pulls off their oily,
translucent wings.

. . . . . . . . . . . . . . .

Emerge from the sand storm
that whips your eyes closed.
The stars are just used-up light.
Believe in something new.

. . . . . . . . . . . . . . .

The sound gets louder and then it stops.

. . . . . . . . . . . . . . .

We consider painting the shells and dressing them as dolls.
A New York artist did that once with cockroaches.
We also consider burning them.

. . . . . . . . . . . . . . .

Depleted uranium
makes the weapons heavy.
What was it that got used up?

. . . . . . . . . . . . . . .

"I don't like the sun," says the eleven-year-old.
I forget to ask her why.

. . . . . . . . . . . . . . .

I sweep one out from the dust of last winter.
It clings to a stick,
the shape of memory.

. . . . . . . . . . . . . . .

After the war,
who will bring the water?

## Gorilla Girl

The gorilla presses his flat face against the bars of his cage at the
Lincoln Park Zoo
and looks directly at me,
ignoring the others who scream and wave.
His eyes go dark and calm.
He holds my gaze.

I'm twelve and it's summer—
vacation time in Chicago at my great aunt's,
whose place smells so strongly of mothballs
that it's entered her cooking.  I imagine
her meat and chicken preserved all these years for infrequent
guests.

After dinner I go to the movies with the ugly cousin.
A zombie springs from a casket,
haunts my dreams for years.

So I celebrate when I read that my gorilla has escaped.
He's sprung himself,
roaming the neighborhood.
It takes days to recapture him.

I think before I was human I was a gorilla too.
Dark, hairy—my night thoughts velvet and strong.
Back all those years, that first woman
silences her baby and teaches us the first word—"shhhhhhh"—
drawing it out long like a snake hissing.

So I still listen,
through daughters and granddaughters,
looking for an inhuman strength
to break the bars;
hiding the silky hairs
that trail down the small of my back.

## Plastic Penguins under Carport

In all likelihood they come from a southern land,
with the lethal extension cords,
lead-bound: *wash hands*
*thoroughly after use.*

Wash hands thoroughly of toxic factories,
of babies with six toes, no longer considered lucky,
of old men with lost legs chanting a mimicry of blessings.

One penguin raises its hat
in a New Year's salute.
Unplugged, the yellow eyes of jaundice
or malaria
are magnets of unseen pain.

In all likelihood a woman wove them,
tying each black strand
of streamer onto the metal frame
to decorate my season
of clean hands.

**Jay**

The jay insistent outside the window
arouses piles of laundry,
the dirty dishes cracked.
The apartment floats past roaches
humming their wings like Kafka.
Some gray, others striped with yellow.
The insistent children grow older
but refuse to dress themselves
or take out the garbage.
They are jealous of life,
want to keep it all,
hoarding the smells
that drove Swift mad.
Japanese cherry and space shuttle bloom together.
This, outside.
Dirty clothes define their own time.
Fold up the angles of sun.

**The Sorcerer's Daughter**

First of all he built that dark tower
And then all that talk about "salamanders" and "gnomes"
While my kohlrabi wilted and the tomatoes developed deep scars.
Dreary daddy stayed lost in his spells.
All I wanted were the vegetables—potatoes, rutabagas and tiny
green peas.
How was I to know he was arranging my marriage?

This morning the Radish-King entered my door
Shrugging his shoulders,
"Bite off a piece.
It tastes like pink ice."

**Elephant**

He tells me I walk like an elephant in the rain.
Later he will cook tandoori chicken in my grandmother's oven
while she hovers astonished at the scent of turmeric.

We eat in the basement where he recognizes ghosts.
As children we ran from the gigantic frog that seemed to live there,
among old shoes and spider webs.

I've always been a seeker of warm rains,
sitting on dampened sheets during heat waves,
drinking the fragrant jasmine tea.

The elephant's eyes are nearly invisible at first—
gray within gray folds of skin.
The office secretary is collecting them.
Clay, marble and glass forms dance across her desk,
the dim scenery of a grafted life.

An elephant rises in my dream.
I follow a trail like Africa,
deeper than words,
the tail rhythmic, sweeping,
just inches above the drying dust.

## Sea Lion

The fat one is sleeping
as the others leap in and out around him.
Near the Embarcadero,
I sit on grass sloping towards water
irrelevant to the sea world.

I think of Chinese soldiers lost to the dust—
mock armies to protect an emperor—
his fear overwhelming the labor of years.
He would die within that earth-bound battle.

On the rock the male sea lion opens one eye,
sees the landscape.
I am the period.
He groans and turns toward the sun.

The others dance in lust on the rock.
Their mobile bodies scatter sea spray
almost reaching me if the wind is right.

The large one will stay
into the night insisting
on capturing the last warmth,
his mouth widening towards
a solitary undefeated yawn.

## Denali Autumn

The brown bears scoop up salmon.
Lined up across the stream they wait
as the fish reach the rapids,
going upstream.
Only one bear is turned wrong,
watches a single spot
for fish coming down.
The rest eat around her
while she sits for hours without motion,
become stone in the eddies of stream.

In first grade I knew a girl named Rosemary.
No one talked to her.
In the school photograph I was forced to stand by her.
Just the two of us,
the outcasts of Edison Elementary.
Her red winter coat is faded wool.
I am hiding my hands in my fancy fur muff,
not wanting to meet anyone halfway.

One bear waits
for the fish that won't jump in her mouth.
More intent than the others
or maybe
not as hungry.

I'm looking for the old photo.
Rosemary had dark hair.
She looked Italian.
Our family album made no
room for her.
My mother excised all pictures of strangers.
My father hid them under his mattress.

## Walleye

You hover like a bat
glued to the un-tiled ceiling.
Among the hidden beams of dream structures
you lurk to remind me
of forgotten promises,
the value of sex.

In the dim dream your voice goes hollow.
I've left the night radio running
and there's interference from walleye fishermen on the Maumee.
They've waded in,
 thigh-high against the current.
They bob from a distance,
their insistent hooks.

Your arms reach and then you pause,
remembering your own death,
quiet and removed.
In another time you whisper of Thoreau,

the young pencil seller.
He couldn't take it either,
this office life we flicker into
like a backwards movie.

In the dream your voice chokes.
You weren't looking for me anyway.
There's no way you could have known
of the gray dawn outdoors—
each fisherman's desire
for the larger fish, heavier to hold.
Silver scales come loose in the early spring rain.

**Just a small dog rescued from the rain**

Tonight I start to know I am dying
not the way you would know, thinking it
but somehow I sense a separation
so I won't stop looking
looking and you know
although I am not allowed
and too weak to jump
you lift me up
one last time to sleep there
curled up by the warmth of your legs.

**The First to Die**


The first to die will be the coral reef,
All color lost, white bone beneath the sea.
Dead zones expand, the creatures of the deep
Grow breathless, struggle long and silently.

All color lost, white bone beneath the sea,
A message for the future's rising shore.
Grown breathless, struggling long and silently,
The gliding birds now lack the strength to soar.

A message for the future's rising shore:
Oil rigs that leak, the asphalt's searing heat.
The gliding birds now lack the strength to soar,
Diminished wings with ever slowing beat.

Oil rigs that leak, the asphalt's searing heat,
A refugee unable to find home,
Diminished wings with ever slowing beat,
Just wind-blown ashes floating in the foam.

A refugee unable to find home,
The forests now a pile of tinder sticks,
Just wind-blown ashes floating in the foam.
Still children look for stars within the rifts.

The forests now a pile of tinder sticks,
All color lost, white bone beneath the sea.
Still children look for stars within the rifts.
The first to die will be the coral reef.

Skaidrite Stelzer is an award-winning poet and two-time Pushcart Prize nominee currently living in Toledo, Ohio, where she teaches a variety of writing and literature classes at The University of Toledo. She has published widely in literary journals as well as in anthologies.

Born in Berchtesgaden, Germany, Skaidrite Stelzer spent her early years in a post-war refugee camp before emigrating to Kalamazoo, Michigan, as a displaced person. Most of her life was lived as a true citizen of the world, with no real home country.

Her interest in poetry began at age four when she memorized a poem in Latvian (her first language), about a freezing angel. Although her original audience was simply her family members, the poem nonetheless resulted in a life-long interest in the power of words. She strives to allow this power to build new connections between language, readers, and multiple experiences.

www.ingramcontent.com/pod-product-compliance
Lightning Source LLC
LaVergne TN
LVHW041515070426
835507LV00012B/1598